Air Fryer Cookbook

Quick, Easy and Delicious Air Fryer Recipes for Healthy and No-Fuss Cooking

Christopher Lester

Table of Contents

Introduction

The use of an air fryer is a new way of frying food, and a much better way when compared with deep frying. This new technology is a healthy way to cook a variety of meals — **breakfasts, poultry, fish and other seafood, meat, sides and vegetables, appetizers and snacks, desserts** — all conveniently prepared in your kitchen.

Food made with air fryers gives the same **crisp, crunch, and flavor** as traditional fried food, and yet it's better for you since the excess fat is eliminated because little or no oil is needed in air fryers. So, you can enjoy most any of your favorite, delicious meals with an air fryer appliance. **Anything you can cook in a conventional oven, you can cook in air fryer.** And, air fryers give more cooking options than the oven. You can use to use them to bake or roast without ever turning on your oven. Use your air fryer to cook fish fillets - like salmon —within minutes; white or sweet potato French fries are crispier; and the high heat treatment of vegetables renders better results.

On top of the appliance, you will see the settings, heating element, and the fan. The basket is located at the bottom and pulls out like a drawer.

In the following sections, you can see: How an Air Fryer Works, Benefits, Maintenance, and Tips for Using Air Fryers.

What Is an Air Fryer and How Does It Work?

An air fryer is basically an amped-up countertop convection oven. It is a **kitchen appliance used for frying foods** like meat, potato chips, and pastries in a healthier way. It's a mini-convention oven used to fry foods, and it gives the same taste and texture as deep-fried foods, but minus all the fat and all those extra calories.

How Does an Air Fryer Work?

An air fryer uses air heated to a given temperature and blows it above and around food and converts moisture into the mist. The heated chamber allows dry heat to penetrate the food from the outside to deep inside the food, which gives the same crispy texture obtained from deep fried food. A chemical reaction is caused—called the Maillard effect—which is a reaction between a decreasing sugar and an amino acid in the presence of heat. This reaction causes the food to change color and flavor.

The hot air blown inside the cooking chamber is blown in all directions, which ensures that food is cooked evenly from every side.

An air fryer is different from the oven because air moves faster in air fryers than it does in a conventional oven. The cooking chamber of an air fryer is confined, so the food also gets done in a short time. Air fried food is healthier than deep-fried foods because of the lower fat and calorie content. Instead of submerging the food entirely in oil, air frying just needs a little drop of oil to give a similar texture and taste like deep-fried foods. Some air fryer manufacturers boast that air fryers can reduce the fat content of fried food by up to 75%.

You can cook basically anything meant to taste deep-fried in an air fryer. Whatever a conventional oven can do, an air fryer can do—just better!

Benefits of an Air Fryer

There are a lot of advantages to using an air fryer over other cooking methods. They include:

1. **Quicker Meals**

Since the cooking chamber is smaller compared to a conventional oven and air is circulated with a fan, food gets done faster. Cooking with an oven might take 20-30 minutes to preheat, but air fryers reach desired high temperatures within minutes of turning it on.

2. **Healthier Cooking**

Cooking oil contains a lot of unhealthy constituents. With an air fryer, you can cook with little oil, and often with no oil at all. You can cook onion rings, frozen fries, wings, and much more, and you will still get the same crispy texture just as if you had used oil

3. Versatility

With an air fryer, the options are endless. Compared to an oven, it fries better and healthier. It can roast, bake, broil, fry, and even grill. You can cook frozen and fresh foods, and also warm leftover foods in them.

4. Space Saver

Compared to other kitchen appliances, air fryers do not take up much space. All that is required is a small space on the counter, and you can quickly move or store it away if needed.

5. Ease of Use

Air fryers are so easy to use: just plug in, add food, select your cooking temperature and cooking time, and start cooking. Shake while cooking; there is no need to stir like it's done using the stove top.

6. Ease of Clean-Up

All you have to clean with an air fryer is the basket and the pan. With ones that have a non-stick coated pan, foods don't get stuck to it and generally easily slide off. A few minutes is all you need, and all the cleaning is done.

7. Energy Efficiency

These fryers are more efficient than using an oven, and they won't heat up your house either. If you intend to save on your electric bill or are worried about the temperature when you cook, an air fryer is an appliance for you.

Maintenance of an Air Fryer

An air fryer is a great appliance to keep in your kitchen as it certainly makes cooking easier. Not only is it simple to use, but it also makes food very convenient. But to ensure the longevity of this appliance, some basic maintenance needs to be done to make sure it doesn't start malfunctioning or get damaged. This includes:

- Ensure that your air fryer is not placed close to another appliance or the wall. For safety and efficiency, air fryers require at least four inches of space around them, both above and beside. This space is needed so that vapor can be appropriately released while cooking. Putting them in a confined space might cause them to overheat.

- Make sure that the cord is in nice shape before plugging in. Plugging a damaged plug into an outlet might cause sparks which could lead to a kitchen fire, an injury, or even a fatality. Make sure the cable isn't damaged or the wires exposed before using your air fryer.

- Carefully check every part of the air fryer. Parts to take note of before each usage include: the frying pan, basket, and even the handle. If you locate any broken pieces, contact the store where you bought it or the manufacturer to get them replaced.

- Make sure the air fryer is placed upright, on a flat surface, before you start food preparation.

- Make sure the appliance is in good, clean condition and free from debris before you start preparing food in it. If it's been long since you last used it, check carefully as it might have collected some dirt over time. Just in case there may be a food deposit or other dirt on the pan or basket, it is best to always clean before you start cooking.

1. **Don't overpack the basket (the cooking chamber).** You might be tempted to save time by overpacking the basket, but this is counterproductive in the long term. Overpacking the basket will not give the crispiness and browning that is needed, and thus will end up using more time.

2. **Add little water to the air fryer drawer when cooking fatty foods.** Adding some water to the drawer just under the basket helps to prevent oil from getting too hot and smoking. This can be done when cooking sausage, bacon, and burgers, for example. This particular tip is applicable when cooking any fatty foods.

3. **Use toothpicks to secure lightweight foods.** Every once in a while, the fan from the air fryer will pick up light foods and blow them around. So, secure light foods with toothpicks.

4. **Occasionally open the air fryer to check for doneness.** This is another thing that makes air fryers lovely. The drawer can be opened as many times as you like to test whatever you are cooking. This will not disturb the programmed time, as most air fryers will either pause heating as you pull out the drawer and then continue when you return the basket, or, continue heating and take note of the time.

5. **Spray with oil during cooking.** If you want a more brown and crisp food, then spritzing with oil during cooking will give you that result. This will also ensure the food browns more evenly.

6. **Turn foods over halfway through the cooking time.** Just as if you were cooking on a grill or deep frying, you need to turn foods over so that they brown evenly.

7. **Shake the basket.** Shaking the basket several times during the cooking process will re-distribute the ingredients and help them to brown and crisp more evenly.

Breakfast Recipes

Asparagus & Bacon Spears

Servings: 4　|　Temperature: 380°F

Prep Time: 15 minutes　|　Cook Time: 8 minutes

INGREDIENTS:

- 20 spears asparagus
- 4 bacon slices
- 1 tablespoon olive oil
- 1 tablespoon sesame oil
- 1 garlic clove, crushed

DIRECTIONS:

1. Pre-heat your Air Fryer to 380 ° F

2. Take a small bowl and add oil, crushed garlic, and mix

3. Separate asparagus into 4 bunches and wrap them in bacon

4. Brush wraps with oil and garlic mix, transfer to your Air Fryer basket

5. Cook for 8 minutes

6. Serve and enjoy!

NUTRITIONAL CONTENTS:

Calories: 175　　　　　　　　Total Carbs: 6
Total Fat: 15g　　　　　　　　Fiber: 2g
Saturated Fat: 4g　　　　　　　Sugar: 2g
Cholesterol: 15mg　　　　　　　Protein: 5g
Sodium: 327mg　　　　　　　　Potassium: 280mg

Tender Potato Pancakes

Servings: 4 | Temperature: 390°F

Prep Time: 10 minutes | Cook Time: 24 minutes

INGREDIENTS:

- 4 medium potatoes, peeled and cleaned
- 1 medium onion, chopped
- 1 beaten egg
- ¼ cup milk
- 2 tablespoons unsalted butter
- ½ teaspoon garlic powder

- ¼ teaspoon salt
- 3 tablespoons all-purpose flour
- Pepper as needed

DIRECTIONS:

1. Peel your potatoes and shred them up.

2. Soak the shredded potatoes under cold water to remove starch.

3. Drain the potatoes.

4. Take a bowl and add eggs, milk, butter, garlic powder, salt, and pepper.

5. Add in flour.

6. Mix well.

7. Add the shredded potatoes.

8. Pre-heat your air fryer to 390°F.

9. Add ¼ cup of the potato pancake batter to your cooking basket and cook for 12 minutes until the golden brown texture is seen.

NUTRITIONAL CONTENTS:

Calories: 248
Total Fat: 11g
Saturated Fat: 3g
Cholesterol: 53mg
Sodium: 470mg

Total Carbs: 33g
Fiber: 1g
Sugar: 3g
Protein: 6g
Potassium: 672mg

Bacon Egg Muffins

Servings: 2 | Temperature: 200°F

Prep Time: 5 minutes | Cook Time: 7 minutes

INGREDIENTS:

- 1 whole egg
- 2 streaky bacon
- 1 English muffin
- Salt and pepper to taste

DIRECTIONS:

1. Pre-heat your Air Fryer to 200°F.

2. Take an oven proof bowl and crack in the egg.

3. Take Air Fryer cooking basket and add bacon, egg, and muffin into Fryer.

4. Cook for 7 minutes.

5. Assemble muffin done by packing bacon and egg on top of English muffin.

6. Serve and enjoy!

NUTRITIONAL CONTENTS:

Calories: 683
Total Fat: 48g
Saturated Fat: 9g
Cholesterol: 416mg
Sodium: 552mg

Total Carbs: 38g
Fiber: 1g
Sugar: 1g
Protein: 24g
Potassium: 227mg

Air Fryer Baked Cheesy Eggs

Servings: 2 | Temperature: 180°F

Prep Time: 10 minutes | Cook Time: 10 minutes

INGREDIENTS:

- 2 whole eggs
- 2 tablespoons milk
- 1 teaspoon parmesan cheese
- 1 tomato, chopped
- Salt and pepper to taste
- 1 bacon slice
- Parsley, chopped for garnish

DIRECTIONS:

1. Pre-heat your oven to 180°F.

2. Cook bacon in a skillet over medium-high heat (with a little bit of oil).

3. Cut bacon into small pieces and divide them equally amongst two ramekins.

4. Dice tomatoes and add them to the ramekins.

5. Add a tablespoon of milk onto each ramekin.

6. Crack an egg into each ramekin.

7. Season both with salt and pepper.

8. Sprinkle ½ teaspoon parmesan into ramekins.

9. Place ramekins into Air Fryer cooking basket and cook for 7 minutes.

10. Serve with a garnish of parsley and enjoy!

NUTRITIONAL CONTENTS:

Calories: 179
Total Fat: 11g
Saturated Fat: 2g
Cholesterol: 186mg
Sodium: 239mg

Total Carbs: 13g
Fiber: 1g
Sugar: 2g
Protein: 8g
Potassium: 208mg

Smoked Bacon & Spinach Bowl

Servings: 4 | Temperature: 392°F

Prep Time: 5 minutes | Cook Time: 10 minutes

INGREDIENTS:

- 8 chestnut mushrooms
- 8 tomatoes, halved
- 1 garlic clove, crushed
- 4 rashers smoked back bacon
- 7 ounces baby leaf spinach
- 4 whole eggs
- Chipotle as needed

DIRECTIONS:

1. Pre-heat your air fryer to 392°F.

2. Take the air fryer cooking basket and add mushrooms, tomatoes, and garlic.

3. Spray with oil and season well.

4. Add bacon, chipotle to the air fryer and cook for 10 minutes.

5. Take a microwave proof bowl and add spinach, heat until wilt.

6. Crack the eggs to the bowl and fry for 2-3 minutes at 320°F.

7. Serve cooked eggs with bacon, enjoy!

NUTRITIONAL CONTENTS:

Calories: 341
Total Fat: 27g
Saturated Fat: 9g
Cholesterol: 61mg
Sodium: 655mg

Total Carbs: 12g
Fiber: 1g
Sugar: 9g
Protein: 13g
Potassium: 430mg

Air Fried Mac & Cheese

Servings: 2 | Temperature: 400°F

Prep Time: 10 minutes | Cook Time: 10 minutes

INGREDIENTS:

- 1 cup elbow macaroni
- ½ cup broccoli
- ½ cup warm milk
- 1½ cheddar cheese, grated
- Salt and pepper to taste
- 1 tablespoon parmesan cheese, grated

DIRECTIONS:

1. Pre-heat your Fryer to 400°F.

2. Take a pot and add water, allow it to boil.

3. Add macaroni and broccoli and broil for about 10 minutes until the mixture is Al Dente.

4. Drain the pasta and vegetables.

5. Toss the Past and veggies with cheese.

6. Season with some pepper and salt and transfer the mixture to your Fryer.

7. Sprinkle some more parmesan on top and cook for about 15 minutes.

8. Allow it to cool for about 10 minutes once done.

9. Enjoy!

NUTRITIONAL CONTENTS:

Calories: 183
Total Fat: 11g
Saturated Fat: 6g
Cholesterol: 50mg
Sodium: 147mg

Total Carbs: 14g
Fiber: 1g
Sugar: 2g
Protein: 6g
Potassium: 59mg

Poultry Recipes

Egg Chicken Escallops

Servings: 6 | Temperature: 392°F

Prep Time: 5 minutes | Cook Time: 5-10 minutes

INGREDIENTS:

- 4 skinless chicken breasts
- 2½ ounces panko breadcrumbs
- 1-ounce parmesan, grated
- 6 sage leaves, chopped
- 1¾ ounces plain flour
- 2 eggs, beaten

DIRECTIONS:

1. Take cling paper and wrap chicken with cling wrap.

2. Beat into ½ cm thickness using a rolling pin.

3. In separate bowls, place parmesan, sage, breadcrumbs, flour and beaten eggs (each ingredient in the separate bowl).

4. Take chicken and dredge into flour, eggs, breadcrumbs and finally parmesan.

5. Pre-heat your fryer to 392°F.

6. Take the basket out and spray chicken with oil on both sides.

7. Cook chicken for 5 minutes each side until golden.

8. Serve and enjoy!

NUTRITIONAL CONTENTS:

Calories: 262
Total Fat: 19g
Saturated Fat: 5g
Cholesterol: 95mg
Sodium: 174mg

Total Carbs: 3g
Fiber: 2g
Sugar: 0g
Protein: 19g
Potassium: 266mg

Creamy Onion Chicken

Servings: 4 | Temperature: 400°F

Prep Time: 30 minutes | Cook Time: 30 minutes

INGREDIENTS:

- 4 chicken breasts
- 1½ cup onion soup mix
- 1 cup mushroom soup
- ½ cup cream

DIRECTIONS:

1. Pre-heat your air fryer to 400°F.

2. Take a frying pan and place it over low heat, add mushrooms, onion mix, and cream.

3. Heat for 1 minute.

4. Pour warm mixture over chicken and let it sit for 25 minutes.

5. Transfer marinated chicken to air fryer and cook for 30 minutes.

6. Serve with a drizzle of remaining cream, enjoy!

NUTRITIONAL CONTENTS:

Calories: 590
Total Fat: 22g
Saturated Fat: 11g
Cholesterol: 72mg
Sodium: 845mg

Total Carbs: 66g
Fiber: 4g
Sugar: 7g
Protein: 25g
Potassium: 686mg

Cheesy Chicken

Servings: 6　　|　　Temperature: 390°F

Prep Time: 10 minutes　　|　　Cook Time: 10 minutes

INGREDIENTS:

- 2 piece (6 ounces each) chicken breast, fat trimmed and sliced up in half
- 6 tablespoons seasoned breadcrumbs
- 2 tablespoons parmesan, grated
- 1 tablespoon melted butter
- 2 tablespoons low-fat mozzarella cheese
- ½ cup marinara sauce
- Cooking spray as needed

DIRECTIONS:

1. Pre-heat your Air Fryer to 390°F for about 9 minutes.

2. Take the cooking basket and spray it evenly with cooking spray.

3. Take a small bowl and add breadcrumbs and parmesan cheese.

4. Mix them well.

5. Take another bowl and add the butter, melt it in your microwave.

6. Brush the chicken pieces with the butter and dredge them into the breadcrumb mix.

7. Once the fryer is ready, place 2 pieces of your prepared chicken breast and spray the top a bit of oil.

8. Cook for about 6 minutes.

9. Turn them over and top them up with 1 tablespoon of Marinara sauce and 1½ tablespoon of shredded mozzarella.

10. Cook for 3 minutes more until the cheese has completely melted.

11. Keep the cooked breasts on the side and repeat with the remaining pieces.

NUTRITIONAL CONTENTS:

Calories: 266
Total Fat: 14g
Saturated Fat: 6g
Cholesterol: 84mg
Sodium: 405mg

Total Carbs: 22g
Fiber: 3g
Sugar: 3g
Protein: 12g
Potassium: 187mg

Honey Chicken Drumsticks

Servings: 2 | Temperature: 400°F

Prep Time: 5 minutes | Cook Time: 15 minutes

INGREDIENTS:

- 2 chicken drumstick, skin removed
- 2 teaspoons olive oil
- 2 teaspoons honey
- ½ teaspoon garlic, minced

DIRECTIONS:

1. Take a resealable zip bag and add olive oil, garlic, and honey, mix well.

2. Add chicken to the bag and let it marinate for 30 minutes.

3. Pre-heat your air fryer to 30 minutes.

4. Transfer chicken to air fryer cooking basket and cook for 15 minutes.

5. Serve and enjoy!

NUTRITIONAL CONTENTS:

Calories: 481
Total Fat: 28g
Saturated Fat: 7g
Cholesterol: 245mg
Sodium: 763mg

Total Carbs: 5g
Fiber: 1g
Sugar: 4g
Protein: 49g
Potassium: 610mg

Spicy Chicken Wings

Servings: 4 | Temperature: 400°F

Prep Time: 3 minutes | Cook Time: 30 minutes

INGREDIENTS:

- 4 pounds chicken wings
- ½ cup cayenne pepper sauce
- ½ cup coconut oil
- 1 tablespoon Worcestershire sauce
- 1 teaspoon salt

DIRECTIONS:

1. Take a mixing cup and add cayenne pepper sauce, coconut oil, Worcestershire sauce, and salt.

2. Mix well and keep it on the side.

3. Pat the chicken dry and transfer to your fryer.

4. Cook for 25 minutes at 380°F, making sure to shake the basket once.

5. Increase the temperature to 400°F and cook for 5 minutes more.

6. Remove them and dump into a large sized mixing bowl.

7. Add the prepared sauce and toss well.

8. Serve with celery sticks and enjoy!

NUTRITIONAL CONTENTS:

Calories: 244
Total Fat: 20g
Saturated Fat: 8g
Cholesterol: 53mg
Sodium: 366mg

Total Carbs: 7g
Fiber: 0g
Sugar: 4g
Protein: 8g
Potassium: 141mg

Buttermilk Spicy Chicken

Servings: 4 | Temperature: 400°F

Prep Time: 20 minutes | Cook Time: 20 minutes

INGREDIENTS:

- 6 chicken thigh, skin on and bone in
- 2 cups buttermilk
- 2 teaspoons salt
- 1 teaspoon cayenne pepper
- 2 cups all-purpose flour

- 1 tablespoon baking powder
- 1 tablespoon garlic powder
- 1 tablespoon paprika
- 1 tablespoon salt

DIRECTIONS:

1. Rinse chicken thoroughly and pat them dry, making sure to remove any fat residue.

2. Take a large bowl and add paprika, pepper, salt, and the chicken. Toss to coat the chicken.

3. Add buttermilk over chicken and cover it well.

4. Let it chill overnight.

5. Pre-heat your air fryer to 400°F.

6. Take a bowl and add flour, paprika, pepper, and salt.

7. Coat the chicken with the flour mix.

8. Transfer chicken to the fryer in a single layer.

9. Cook for 10 minutes.

10. Do in batches if needed, serve and enjoy!

NUTRITIONAL CONTENTS:

Calories: 251
Total Fat: 14g
Saturated Fat: 5g
Cholesterol: 81mg
Sodium: 356mg

Total Carbs: 5g
Fiber: 0g
Sugar: 2g
Protein: 25g
Potassium: 303mg

Honey & Orange Chicken

Servings: 4 | Temperature: 400°F

Prep Time: 30 minutes | Cook Time: 30 minutes

INGREDIENTS:

- 1½ pounds chicken breast
- Parsley to taste
- 1 cup coconut
- ¼ cup coconut oil
- ¾ cup breadcrumbs
- 2 whole eggs

- ½ cup flour
- Salt to taste
- ½ cup orange marmalade
- 1 teaspoon red pepper flakes
- ¼ cup honey
- 3 tablespoons Dijon mustard

DIRECTIONS:

1. Pre-heat your air fryer to 400°F.

2. Wash your chicken thoroughly and cut into slices.

3. Take a bowl and blend in coconut, breadcrumbs, flour, salt, parsley, and pepper.

4. Take another plate and add eggs.

5. Take a frying pan and place it over medium heat, add coconut oil and let it heat up.

6. Dredge the chicken in egg mix, flour and then with panko.

7. Transfer prepared chicken to your air fryer and bake for 15 minutes.

8. Take a bowl and mix in honey, marmalade, mustard and pepper flakes.

9. Cover chicken with marmalade mix and cook for 5 minutes more.

10. Serve and enjoy!

NUTRITIONAL CONTENTS:

Calories: 643
Total Fat: 26g
Saturated Fat: 7g
Cholesterol: 150mg
Sodium: 754mg

Total Carbs: 55g
Fiber: 2g
Sugar: 29g
Protein: 49g
Potassium: 871mg

Cheesy Chicken Cutlets

Servings: 4 | Temperature: 400°F

Prep Time: 20 minutes | Cook Time: 25 minutes

INGREDIENTS:

- ¼ cup parmesan
- 4 chicken breasts
- 1/8 teaspoon paprika
- ¼ teaspoon pepper

- 2 tablespoons panko breadcrumbs
- 1 teaspoon parsley
- ½ teaspoon garlic powder
- 1 bread loaf

DIRECTIONS:

1. Pre-heat your air fryer to 400°F.

2. Take a bowl and mix in parmesan and panko.

3. Mix in garlic powder, pepper, paprika.

4. Mix well.

5. Wash and cut your chicken breasts.

6. Take a bowl and add water, take another bowl and add bread to the bowl. Gently mash it.

7. Cover chicken with panko mix and form chicken cutlets.

8. Add bread to your chicken cutlet and transfer cutlets to air fryer.

9. Cook for 25 minutes.

10. Serve and enjoy!

NUTRITIONAL CONTENTS:

Calories: 703
Total Fat: 45g
Saturated Fat: 9g
Cholesterol: 181mg
Sodium: 585mg

Total Carbs: 36g
Fiber: 2g
Sugar: 1g
Protein: 38g
Potassium: 385mg

Bread Chicken Tenders

Servings: 4 | Temperature: 330°F

Prep Time: 10 minutes | Cook Time: 15 minutes

INGREDIENTS:

- ¾ pound chicken tenders

For Breading

- 2 whole eggs, beaten
- ½ cup seasoned breadcrumbs
- ½ cup all-purpose flour

- 1 teaspoon pepper
- 2 tablespoons olive oil

DIRECTIONS:

1. Pre-heat your fryer to 330°F.

2. Take three bowls and add breadcrumbs, eggs, and flour individually.

3. Season the breadcrumbs with salt and pepper.

4. Add olive oil to the breadcrumbs and mix well.

5. Dredge the chicken tenders into the flour, eggs and finally In the breadcrumbs.

6. Take out your crumb covered tendered and place them in your air fryer cooking basket.

7. Cook for 10 minutes.

8. Increase the temperature to 390°F and cook for 5 minutes more.

9. Enjoy!

NUTRITIONAL CONTENTS:

Calories: 149
Total Fat: 6g
Saturated Fat: 1g
Cholesterol: 27mg
Sodium: 328mg

Total Carbs: 18g
Fiber: 1g
Sugar: 6g
Protein: 6g
Potassium: 116mg

Fish & Seafood Recipes

Fish Cake & Mango Salsa

Servings: 4 | Temperature: 352°F

Prep Time: 20 minutes | Cook Time: 14 minutes

INGREDIENTS:

- 1 ripe mango
- 1½ teaspoon red chili paste
- 3 tablespoons fresh coriander
- 1 lime juice
- 1 pound fish fillet
- 2 ounces shredded coconut

DIRECTIONS:

1. Peel the mango and cut it up into small cubes.

2. Mix the mango cubes in a bowl alongside ½ a teaspoon of red chili paste, juice, zest of lime and 1 tablespoon of coriander.

3. Puree the fish in a food processor and mix with 1 teaspoon of salt and 1 egg.

4. Add the rest of the lime zest, lime juice, and red chili paste.

5. Mix well alongside the remaining coriander.

6. Add 2 tablespoon of coconut and green onion.

7. Put the rest of the coconut on a soup plate.

8. Divide the fish mixture into 12 portions and shape them into cakes.

9. Coat with coconut.

10. Place six of the cakes in your fryer and cook for 8 minutes until they are golden brown at 352°F.

11. Repeat until all cakes are used up.

12. Serve with mango salsa.

NUTRITIONAL CONTENTS:

Calories: 153
Total Fat: 6g
Saturated Fat: 1g
Cholesterol: 54mg
Sodium: 36mg

Total Carbs:16g
Fiber: 2g
Sugar: 1g
Protein: 8g
Potassium: 459mg

Cheesy Salmon

Servings: 6 | Temperature: 356°F

Prep Time: 5 minutes | Cook Time: 7 minutes

INGREDIENTS:

- 1 bunch basil
- 2 garlic cloves
- 1 tablespoon olive oil (for cooking)
- ¼ cup olive oil (extra)
- 1 tablespoon parmesan cheese
- Salt and pepper to taste
- 2 tablespoons Pinenuts
- 6 ounces white fish fillet

DIRECTIONS:

1. Drizzle the fish fillets with oil and season with some pepper and salt.

2. Preheat your air fryer to 356°F.

3. Carefully transfer the fillets to your air fryer cooking basket.

4. Cook for about 8 minutes.

5. Take a small bowl and add basil, olive oil, pine nuts, garlic, parmesan cheese and blend using your hand.

6. Serve this mixture with the fish!

NUTRITIONAL CONTENTS:

Calories: 344
Total Fat: 26g
Saturated Fat: 10g
Cholesterol: 68mg
Sodium: 362mg

Total Carbs: 7g
Fiber: 1g
Sugar: 0g
Protein: 21g
Potassium: 417mg

Salmon with Dill Sauce

Servings: 4 | Temperature: 270°F

Prep Time: 10 minutes | Cook Time: 35 minutes

INGREDIENTS:

Salmon

- 4 salmon, each of 6 ounces
- 2 teaspoons olive oil
- 1 pinch salt

Dill Sauce

- ½ cup non-fat Greek yogurt
- ½ cup sour cream
- Pinch of salt
- 2 tablespoons chopped dill

DIRECTIONS:

1. Preheat your air fryer to 270°F.

2. Drizzle cut pieces of salmon with 1 teaspoon olive oil.

3. Season with salt.

4. Take the cooking basket out and transfer salmon to basket, cook for 20-23 minutes.

5. Take a bowl and add sour cream, salt, chopped dill, yogurt and mix well to prepare the dill sauce.

6. Serve cooked salmon by pouring the sauce all over.

7. Garnish with chopped dill and enjoy!

NUTRITIONAL CONTENTS:

Calories: 696
Total Fat: 45g
Saturated Fat: 10g
Cholesterol: 166mg
Sodium: 788mg

Total Carbs: 2g
Fiber: 1g
Sugar: 1g
Protein: 62g
Potassium: 1515mg

Spicy Shrimp

Servings: 4 | Temperature: 390°F

Prep Time: 5 minutes | Cook Time: 7 minutes

INGREDIENTS:

Salmon

- 1¼ pound tiger shrimp, about 16-20 pieces
- ¼ teaspoon cayenne pepper
- ½ teaspoon old bay seasoning
- ¼ teaspoon smoked paprika
- 1 pinch of salt
- 1 tablespoon olive oil

DIRECTIONS:

1. Pre-heat your air fryer to 390°F.

2. Take a mixing bowl and add ingredients (except shrimp), mix well.

3. Dip the shrimp into spice mixture and oil.

4. Transfer the prepared shrimp to your cooking basket and cook for 5 minutes.

5. Serve and enjoy!

NUTRITIONAL CONTENTS:

Calories: 176
Total Fat: 2g
Saturated Fat: 1g
Cholesterol: 214mg
Sodium: 976mg

Total Carbs: 5g
Fiber: 0g
Sugar: 1g
Protein: 23g
Potassium: 251mg

Fish Nuggets

Servings: 6 | Temperature: 390°F

Prep Time: 5 minutes | Cook Time: 10 minutes

INGREDIENTS:

Salmon

- 1 pound fresh cod
- 2 tablespoons olive oil
- ½ cup flour

- 2 large finely beaten eggs
- 3 quarters, panko bread
- Salt as needed

DIRECTIONS:

1. Pre-heat your air fryer to 388°F.

2. Take a food processor and add olive oil, breadcrumbs, salt and blend.

3. Take three bowls and add flour, breadcrumbs, beaten eggs individually.

4. Take cods and cut them into slices of 1-inch thickness and 2-inch length.

5. Dredge slices into flour, eggs and in crumbs.

6. Transfer nuggets to air fryer cooking basket and cook for 10 minutes until golden.

7. Serve and enjoy!

NUTRITIONAL CONTENTS:

Calories: 199
Total Fat: 14g
Saturated Fat: 7g
Cholesterol: 114mg
Sodium: 802mg

Total Carbs: 6g
Fiber: 1g
Sugar: 2g
Protein: 14g
Potassium: 245mg

Meat Recipes

Skirt Steak & Chimichurri Sauce

Servings: 6 | Temperature: 390°F

Prep Time: 30 minutes | Cook Time: 10 minutes

INGREDIENTS:

- 16 ounces skirt steak

Chimichurri Sauce

- 1 cup parsley, chopped
- ¼ cup mint, chopped
- 2 tablespoons oregano, chopped
- 3 garlic cloves, chopped
- 1 teaspoon crushed red pepper
- 1 tablespoon cumin, grounded
- 1 teaspoon cayenne pepper
- 2 teaspoons smoked paprika
- 1 teaspoon salt
- ¼ teaspoon pepper
- ¾ cup olive oil
- 3 tablespoons red wine vinegar

DIRECTIONS:

1. Take a bowl and mix all of the ingredients listed under Chimichurri section and mix them well.

2. Cut the steak into 2 pieces of 8-ounce portions.

3. Take a re-sealable bag and add ¼ cup of Chimichurri alongside the steak pieces and shake

them to ensure that steak is coated well.

4. Chill it in your fridge for 2-24 hours.

5. Remove the steak from the refrigerator 30 minutes before cooking.

6. Pre-heat your fryer to 390°F.

7. Transfer the steak to your fryer and cook for about 8-10 minutes if you are looking for a medium-rare finish.

8. Garnish with 2 tablespoons of Chimichurri sauce and enjoy!

NUTRITIONAL CONTENTS:

Calories: 244
Total Fat: 18g
Saturated Fat: 5g
Cholesterol: 42mg
Sodium: 276mg

Total Carbs: 9g
Fiber: 1g
Sugar: 2g
Protein: 13g
Potassium: 262mg

Air Fried Beef Schnitzel

Servings: 4 | Temperature: 390°F

Prep Time: 10 minutes | Cook Time: 12 minutes

INGREDIENTS:

- 2 tablespoons olive oil
- 2 ounces breadcrumbs
- 1 whisked egg
- 1 thin beef schnitzel
- 1 lemon

DIRECTIONS:

1. Pre-heat your air fryer to 356°F.

2. Take a bowl and add breadcrumbs, oil and mix well.

3. Keep stirring until you have an excellent loose texture.

4. Dip schnitzel into the egg and shake any excess.

5. Dredge coat schnitzel into breadcrumbs and coat them.

6. Layer in fryer basket and cook for 12 minutes.

7. Serve with a garnish of lemon.

8. Enjoy!

NUTRITIONAL CONTENTS:

Calories: 413
Total Fat: 11g
Saturated Fat: 3g
Cholesterol: 114mg
Sodium: 506mg

Total Carbs: 43g
Fiber: 1g
Sugar: 1g
Protein: 33g
Potassium: 590mg

Lamb Chops & Garlic Sauce

Servings: 4 | Temperature: 392°F

Prep Time: 15 minutes | Cook Time: 22 minutes

INGREDIENTS:

- 1 garlic bulb
- 3 tablespoons olive oil
- 1 tablespoon fresh oregano, chopped

- Fresh ground black pepper
- 8 lamb chops

DIRECTIONS:

1. Pre-heat your air fryer to 392°F.

2. Take a garlic bulb and coat with olive oil.

3. Roast bulb for 12 minutes in fryer.

4. Take a bowl and add salt, olive oil, and pepper.

5. Coat lamb chops with ½ tablespoon of herb/oil mix and let it marinate for 5 minutes.

6. Pre-heat your fryer to 392°F.

7. Remove the bulb from coking tray and add lamb to the fryer, cook for 5 minutes.

8. Squeeze garlic clove between your thumb and index finger over the herb oil mix, season with salt and pepper.

9. Serve the lamb chops with garlic sauce.

10. Enjoy!

NUTRITIONAL CONTENTS:

Calories: 379
Total Fat: 35g
Saturated Fat: 15g
Cholesterol: 76mg
Sodium: 245mg

Total Carbs: 1g
Fiber: 0g
Sugar: 0g
Protein: 15g
Potassium: 203mg

Cheddar Bacon

Servings: 4 | Temperature: 390°F

Prep Time: 10 minutes | Cook Time: 30 minutes

INGREDIENTS:

For Breading

- 4 tablespoons olive oil
- 1 cup all-purpose flour

- 2 beaten eggs
- 1 cup seasoned bread crumbs

For Filling

- 1 pound sharp cheddar
- 1 pound thinly sliced bacon, at room temperature

DIRECTIONS:

1. Cut up the cheddar cheese blocks in equal portions of 1 x 1 x ¾ inch portions.

2. Take two pieces of bacon and cover them up with the cheddar, making sure that they are fully engulfed with the bacon.

3. Trim any excess fat.

4. Take the wrapped cheese and place them in your fridge, allow them to chill for 15 minutes.

5. Pre-heat your fryer to 390°F.

6. Take a bowl and add oil and breadcrumbs and mix well.

7. Dredge the wrapped up cheese into flour, eggs, and breadcrumbs.

8. Cook for 7-8 minutes and serve one golden brown texture is seen!

NUTRITIONAL CONTENTS:

Calories: 461
Total Fat: 26g
Saturated Fat: 13g
Cholesterol: 106mg
Sodium: 511mg

Total Carbs: 43g
Fiber: 2g
Sugar: 1g
Protein: 14g
Potassium: 193mg

Herbed Round Roast Beef

Servings: 2 | Temperature: 360°F

Prep Time: 10 minutes | Cook Time: 12 minutes

INGREDIENTS:

- 2 teaspoons olive oil
- 4 pound top round roast beef
- 1 teaspoon salt
- ¼ teaspoon fresh ground black pepper

- 1 teaspoon dried thyme
- ½ teaspoon rosemary, chopped
- 3 pounds red potatoes, halved
- Olive oil, fresh ground black pepper, and salt to taste

DIRECTIONS:

1. Pre-heat your air fryer to 360°F.

2. Rub olive oil all over the beef.

3. Take a bowl and add rosemary, thyme, salt, and pepper.

4. Mix well.

5. Season the beef with the mixture and transfer the meat to your fryer. Cook for 20 minutes.

6. Add potatoes alongside some pepper and oil.

7. Turn the roast alongside and add the potatoes to the basket. Cook for 20 minutes.

8. Make sure to rotate the mixture from time to time.

9. Cook until you have reached your desired temperature (130 F for Rare, 140 F for Medium and 160 F for Well Done).

10. Once done, allow the meat to cool for 10 minutes.

11. Pre-heat your air fryer to 400°F and keep cooking the potatoes for 10 minutes.

12. Serve with the potatoes with the beef and enjoy!

NUTRITIONAL CONTENTS:

Calories: 735
Total Fat: 63g
Saturated Fat: 26g
Cholesterol: 161mg
Sodium: 363mg
Total Carbs: 1g

Fiber: 0g
Sugar: 0g
Protein: 37g
Potassium: 626mg

Macadamia Crusted Roast

Servings: 4 | Temperature: 390°F

Prep Time: 15 minutes | Cook Time: 22 minutes

INGREDIENTS:

- 1 garlic clove
- 1 tablespoon olive oil
- 1¼ pound rack of lamb
- Salt and pepper to taste

Macadamia Crusts

- 3 ounces unsalted macadamia crust
- 1 tablespoon breadcrumbs
- 1 tablespoon fresh rosemary, chopped
- 1 whole egg

DIRECTIONS:

1. Chop up the garlic and toss it with some olive oil to create a garlic oil mix.

2. Brush the lamb rack with this prepared oil.

3. Season with pepper and salt.

4. Pre-heat your air fryer to 220°F.

5. Chop up the macadamia nuts and put them to a bowl.

6. Add breadcrumbs and rosemary, and mix them well.

7. Take another bowl and whisk eggs.

8. Dredge the meat into the egg mix and drain excess egg.

9. Coat the lamb rack with the macadamia crust and place them into the air fryer basket.

10. Cook for about 30 minutes, making sure to increase the temperature of 390°F after 30 minutes.

11. Cook for 5 minutes more.

12. Remove the meat and let it cool.

13. Cover with aluminum foil and leave for 10 minutes.

14. Enjoy!

NUTRITIONAL CONTENTS:

Calories: 301
Total Fat: 31g
Saturated Fat: 5g
Cholesterol: 0mg
Sodium: 114mg

Total Carbs: 7g
Fiber: 1g
Sugar: 3g
Protein: 33g
Potassium: 162mg

Honey Pork Ribs

Servings: 4　|　Temperature: 390°F

Prep Time: 5 minutes　|　Cook Time: 16 minutes

INGREDIENTS:

- 1 pound pork ribs
- 1 teaspoon salt
- 1 teaspoon pepper
- 1 tablespoon sugar

- 1 teaspoon ginger juice
- 1 teaspoon five spice powder
- 1 tablespoon teriyaki sauce
- 1 tablespoon light soy sauce

- 1 garlic clove, minced
- 2 tablespoons honey

- 1 tablespoon water
- 1 tablespoon tomato sauce

DIRECTIONS:

1. Prepare marinade by mixing pepper, sugar, salt, five spice powder, teriyaki sauce, ginger juice and mix well.

2. Rub mixture all over pork and let it marinate for 2 hours.

3. Pre-heat your air fryer to 350°F.

4. Add ribs to your air fryer and cook for 8 minutes.

5. Take a mixing bowl and add soy sauce, garlic, honey, water, and tomato sauce

6. Mix well.

7. Stir-fry the garlic in oil until fragrant

8. Transfer the air-fried pork ribs to the pan with garlic and add sauce

9. Mix and enjoy!

NUTRITIONAL CONTENTS:

Calories: 296
Total Fat: 22g
Saturated Fat: 7g
Cholesterol: 71mg
Sodium: 454mg

Total Carbs: 10g
Fiber: 1g
Sugar: 2g
Protein: 15g
Potassium: 281mg

Bacon & Garlic Platter

Servings: 4 | Temperature: 392°F

Prep Time: 10 minutes | Cook Time: 30 minutes

INGREDIENTS:

- 4 potatoes, halved and peeled
- 6 garlic cloves, unpeeled and squashed
- 4 rashers streaky bacon, roughly cut
- 2 sprigs rosemary
- 1 tablespoon olive oil

DIRECTIONS:

1. Take a bowl and add garlic, bacon, rosemary, and potatoes.

2. Add oil and mix well.

3. Pre-heat your air fryer to 392°F.

4. Transfer mixture to Air Fryer cooking basket and roast for 25-30 minutes.

5. Serve and enjoy!

NUTRITIONAL CONTENTS:

Calories: 282
Total Fat: 14g
Saturated Fat: 8g
Cholesterol: 33mg
Sodium: 527mg

Total Carbs: 34g
Fiber: 1g
Sugar: 3g
Protein: 6g
Potassium: 798mg

Cheesy Bacon Fries

Servings: 4 | Temperature: 400°F and 340°F

Prep Time: 10 minutes | Cook Time: 16 minutes

INGREDIENTS:

- 2 large russet potatoes, peeled and cut into ½ inch strips
- 4 slices bacon, diced
- 2 tablespoons olive oil
- 2½ cups cheddar, cheese
- 3 ounces melted cream cheese
- Salt and pepper to taste
- ¼ cup scallions, chopped
- Ranch dressing if preferred

DIRECTIONS:

1. Put the water to boil.

2. Blanch the potatoes in the salted water for about 4 minutes and strain them in a colander.

3. Rinse them with cold water and remove the starch. Dry potatoes.

4. Heat the fryer to 400° F.

5. Place the chopped bacon into your air fryer and fry for about 4 minutes; shake the basket halfway through.

6. Drain the bacon and discard any excess grease that accumulated in the bottom of the fryer.

7. Toss the dried potato sticks with some oil and place them in the fryer basket.

8. Fry them at 360° F.for 25 minutes; shake the basket from time to time.

9. Season fries with some salt and pepper about halfway through the cooking process.

10. Transfer the fries from your basket to an 8-inch pan.

11. Mix about 2 cups of cheddar cheese with the melted cream cheese.

12. Dollop the cheese mix over the potatoes.

13. Sprinkle some more cheddar cheese over the fries and top them with crumbled bacon.

14. Lower the baking pan into your air fryer's cooking basket using a sling.

15. Air fry it for about 5 minutes at 340° F.

16. Sprinkle some chopped scallions as garnish and serve with your favorite ranch dressing.

NUTRITIONAL CONTENTS:

Calories: 118
Total Fat: 8g
Saturated Fat: 3g
Cholesterol: 31mg
Sodium: 203mg

Total Carbs: 6g
Fiber: 0gch
Sugar: 0g
Protein: 5g
Potassium: 47mg

Sides & Vegetable Recipes

Vegetable Cutlets

Servings: 6 | Temperature: 356°F

Prep Time: 10 minutes | Cook Time: 16 minutes

INGREDIENTS:

- 7 ounces potatoes
- ½ medium carrot, grated
- 2 ounces capsicum, chopped
- 2 ounces cabbage, chopped

- Salt as needed
- Panko breadcrumbs
- 1 teaspoons arrowroot mixed with water

DIRECTIONS:

1. Take a pot of boiling water and add potatoes.

2. Once the potatoes are boiled, take them out and let them cool.

3. Peel the potatoes and mash them alongside cabbage, capsicum and season the mixture with salt.

4. Divide the mixture into 6 balls.

5. Flatten balls into cutlet shapes.

6. Coat each ball with arrowroot slurry and dredge them in breadcrumbs.

7. Pre-heat your fryer to 356°F.

8. Transfer balls to your air fryer cooking basket and cook for 8 minutes, give them a turn and cook for 8 minutes more.

9. Serve and enjoy!

NUTRITIONAL CONTENTS:

Calories: 240
Total Fat: 4g
Saturated Fat: 0g
Cholesterol: 0mg
Sodium: 498mg

Total Carbs: 46g
Fiber: 3g
Sugar: 5g
Protein: 7g
Potassium: 938mg

Cumin & Squash Chili

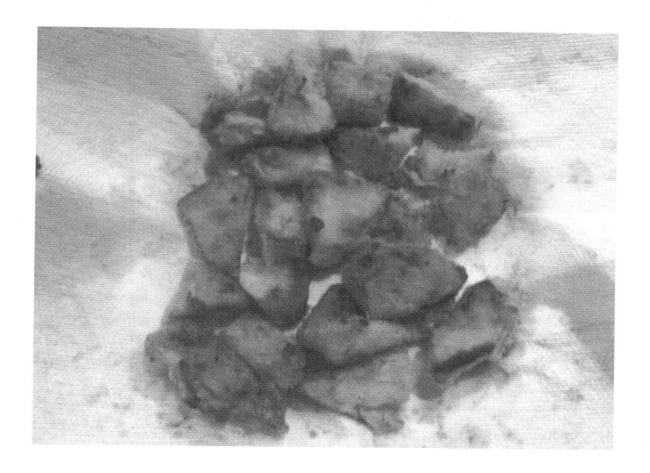

Servings: 6 | Temperature: 360°F

Prep Time: 10 minutes | Cook Time: 16 minutes

INGREDIENTS:

- 1 medium butternut squash
- 2 teaspoons cumin seeds
- 1 large pinch chili flakes

- 1 tablespoon olive oil
- 1½ ounces pine nuts
- 1 small bunch fresh coriander, chopped

DIRECTIONS:

1. Take the squash and slice it.

2. Remove seeds and cut into smaller chunks.

3. Take a bowl and add chunked squash, spice and oil.

4. Mix well.

5. Pre-heat your fryer to 360°F and add the squash to the cooking basket.

6. Roast for 20 minutes, don't forget to shake the basket from time to time to avoid burning.

7. Place the pan over medium heat.

8. Add pine nuts to the pan and dry toast for 2 minutes.

9. Sprinkle nuts on top of squash and serve.

10. Enjoy!

NUTRITIONAL CONTENTS:

Calories: 414
Total Fat: 15g
Saturated Fat: 2g
Cholesterol: 0mg
Sodium: 1378mg

Total Carbs: 58g
Fiber: 22g
Sugar: 7g
Protein: 16g
Potassium: 1370mg

Blooming Onion

Servings: 4 | Temperature: 360°F

Prep Time: 10 minutes | Cook Time: 15 minutes

INGREDIENTS:

- 2 pounds Cippolini onions
- Olive oil as needed
- 2 whole eggs
- 1 teaspoon cayenne pepper

- 1 cup buttermilk
- 1 teaspoon garlic powder
- 2 cups flour
- 1 tablespoon pepper

- 1 tablespoon paprika
- 1 tablespoon salt
- ¼ cup mayonnaise
- 1 tablespoon ketchup
- ¼ cup sour cream

DIRECTIONS:

1. Wash onions thoroughly and clean them well.

2. Cut onion edges and make a flower like a shape (or your favorite shape).

3. In a bowl, carefully mix salt, pepper, salt, paprika, flour, garlic powder, cayenne pepper.

4. Add mayo, ketchup, cream and herb mix, stir well.

5. Transfer onions to a plate with beaten egg, cover the onions with the prepared sauce.

6. Drizzle olive oil on top.

7. Transfer onions to your air fryer basket.

8. Cook for 15 minutes at 360°F.

9. Serve and enjoy!

NUTRITIONAL CONTENTS:

Calories: 122
Total Fat: 1g
Saturated Fat: 0g
Cholesterol: 0mg
Sodium: 289mg

Total Carbs: 23g
Fiber: 2g
Sugar: 4g
Protein: 6g
Potassium: 181mg

Banana Fritters

Servings: 6 | Temperature: 340°F

Prep Time: 10 minutes | Cook Time: 16 minutes

INGREDIENTS:

- 1½ cups flour
- 5 bananas, peeled and sliced
- 1 teaspoon salt
- 1 cup water

DIRECTIONS:

1. Pre-heat your air fryer to 340°F.

2. Take a bowl and add salt, sesame seeds, water and mix them well until nice batter forms.

3. Coat the bananas with the flour mixture and transfer them to the fryer basket.

4. Cook for 8 minutes.

5. Enjoy!

NUTRITIONAL CONTENTS:

Calories: 242
Total Fat: 9g
Saturated Fat: 2g
Cholesterol: 53mg
Sodium: 22mg

Total Carbs: 38g
Fiber: 3g
Sugar: 14g
Protein: 5g
Potassium: 451mg

Avocado Fries

Servings: 6 | Temperature: 390°F

Prep Time: 10 minutes | Cook Time: 20 minutes

INGREDIENTS:

- ½ cup breadcrumbs
- ½ teaspoon salt
- 1 Hass avocado, peeled, pitted and sliced
- Aquafaba from one bean can (bean liquid)

DIRECTIONS:

1. Take a shallow bowl and add breadcrumbs, salt.

2. Pour aquafaba in another bowl, dredge avocado slices in aquafaba and then into the crumbs to get a nice coating.

3. Arrange them in a single layer in your air fryer cooking basket, don't overlap.

4. Cook for 10 minutes at 390°F, give the basket a shake and cook for 5 minutes more.

5. Serve and enjoy!

NUTRITIONAL CONTENTS:

Calories: 356
Total Fat: 14g
Saturated Fat: 2g
Cholesterol: 50mg
Sodium: 344mg

Total Carbs: 34g
Fiber: 3g
Sugar: 2g
Protein: 23g
Potassium: 455mg

Onion Pakora

Servings: 6 | Temperature: 392°F

Prep Time: 5 minutes | Cook Time: 10 minutes

INGREDIENTS:

- 1 cup Gram Flour
- ¼ cup almond flour
- 2 teaspoons olive oil
- 4 whole onion
- 2 whole green chili

- 1 tablespoon coriander
- ¼ teaspoon carom
- 1/8 teaspoon chili powder
- Salt as needed

DIRECTIONS:

1. Slice your onion into individual slices.

2. Chop the green chilies.

3. Cut up the coriander into equal sized portions.

4. Take a bowl and add carom, turmeric powder, salt, and chili powder.

5. Add onion, chilies, and coriander.

6. Mix well.

7. Add water and keep mixing until you have a dough like consistency.

8. Mix the dough and form balls.

9. Pre-heat your fryer to 392°F.

10. Cook for 8 minutes.

11. Make sure to keep checking after every 6 minutes to ensure that they are not burnt.

NUTRITIONAL CONTENTS:

Calories: 282
Total Fat: 18g
Saturated Fat: 1g
Cholesterol: 0mg
Sodium: 353mg

Total Carbs: 23g
Fiber: 4g
Sugar: 5g
Protein: 8g
Potassium: 353mg

Lemon Flavored Green Beans

Servings: 4 | Temperature: 400°F

Prep Time: 5 minutes | Cook Time: 12-15 minutes

INGREDIENTS:

- 1 pound green beans, washed and de-stemmed
- 1 lemon

- Pinch of salt
- ¼ teaspoon oil

DIRECTIONS:

1. Add beans to your air fryer cooking basket.

2. Squeeze a few drops of lemon.

3. Season with salt and pepper.

4. Drizzle olive oil on top.

5. Cook for 10-12 minutes at 400°F.

6. Once done, serve and enjoy!

NUTRITIONAL CONTENTS:

Calories: 84
Total Fat: 5g
Saturated Fat: 1g
Cholesterol: 0mg
Sodium: 309mg

Total Carbs: 9g
Fiber: 3g
Sugar: 4g
Protein: 2g
Potassium: 259mg

Baked Mediterranean Vegetables

Servings: 8 | Temperature: 380°F

Prep Time: 20 minutes | Cook Time: 45 minutes

INGREDIENTS:

- Olive oil, as needed
- 18 ounces eggplant
- 4 garlic cloves
- Bunch of thyme sprig
- 18 ounces bell pepper

- Salt and pepper, to taste
- 4 whole onions
- Bay leaf
- 18 ounces tomatoes
- Breadcrumbs

DIRECTIONS:

1. Pre-heat your air fryer to 380°F.

2. Cut tomatoes in half and bake them in your fryer for 2 minutes.

3. Take a bowl and mix eggplants with olive oil and spices, cook for 4 minutes in the fryer.

4. Drizzle olive oil over zucchini and transfer to air fryer, cook for 4 minutes.

5. Add tomatoes and bell pepper to the fryer (with zucchini) and bake for 2 minutes more, add breadcrumbs and olive oil.

6. Serve and enjoy!

NUTRITIONAL CONTENTS:

Calories: 282
Total Fat: 12g
Saturated Fat: 4g
Cholesterol: 20mg
Sodium: 910mg

Total Carbs: 31g
Fiber: 2g
Sugar: 6g
Protein: 10g
Potassium: 266mg

Parsnip & Potato Bake

Servings: 8 | Temperature: 360°F

Prep Time: 30 minutes | Cook Time: 25 minutes

INGREDIENTS:

- 28 ounces potato
- 3 tablespoons pine nuts
- 28 ounces parsnips
- 1¾ ounces parmesan, coarse
- 6¾ ounces crème Fraiche

- 1 slice bread
- 2 tablespoons sage
- Butter as needed
- 4 teaspoons mustard

DIRECTIONS:

1. Pre-heat your air fryer to 360°F.

2. Take the pot and place it over medium heat, add water, potatoes, and parsnips and boil.

3. Take a bowl and mix mustard, crème, sage, salt, and pepper.

4. Peel the boiled vegetables and mash them.

5. Transfer the mustard mixture to your mashed potatoes and mix well.

6. Mix in panko, cheese, and nuts to the potato mix.

7. Transfer the mixture to your air fryer cooking basket and cook for 25 minutes

8. Serve and enjoy!

NUTRITIONAL CONTENTS:

Calories: 271
Total Fat: 22g
Saturated Fat: 5g
Cholesterol: 49mg
Sodium: 294mg

Total Carbs: 16g
Fiber: 3g
Sugar: 3g
Protein: 3g
Potassium: 329mg

Appetizers & Snacks

Air-Fried Pumpkin Seeds

Servings: 1½ cups | Temperature: 350°F

Prep Time: 10 minutes | Cook Time: 65 minutes

INGREDIENTS:

- 1½ cups pumpkin seeds
- Olive oil as needed
- 1½ teaspoons salt
- 1 teaspoon smoked paprika

DIRECTIONS:

1. Cut pumpkin and scrape out seeds and flesh.

2. Separate flesh from seeds and rinse the seeds under cold water.

3. Bring 2 quarter of salted water to boil and add seeds, simmer for 10 minutes.

4. Drain seeds and spread them on a kitchen towel.

5. Dry for 20 minutes.

6. Pre-heat your fryer to 350°F.

7. Take a bowl and add seeds, smoked paprika, and olive oil.

8. Season with salt and transfer to your air fryer cooking basket.

9. Cook for 35 minutes.

10. Enjoy!

NUTRITIONAL CONTENTS:

Calories: 237
Total Fat: 21g
Saturated Fat: 6g
Cholesterol: 16mg
Sodium: 82mg

Total Carbs: 4g
Fiber: 2g
Sugar: 0g
Protein: 12g
Potassium: 273mg

Potato Wedges

Servings: 6 | Temperature: 352°F

Prep Time: 10 minutes | Cook Time: 20 minutes

INGREDIENTS:

- 26 ounces large waxy potatoes
- 2 tablespoons olive oil
- 2 teaspoons smoked paprika
- 2 tablespoons Sriracha hot chili sauce

DIRECTIONS:

1. Peel potatoes and slice into wedge-like shapes.

2. Soak wedges under water for 30 minutes.

3. Take a towel and dry them.

4. Pre-heat your fryer to 352°F.

5. Coat potatoes with paprika and oil and transfer them to the cooking basket.

6. Cook for 20 minutes, making sure to give the basket a shake.

7. Take the wedges out of the fryer and let them dry.

8. Serve with a seasoning of salt and pepper, over a side of chili sauce.

9. Enjoy!

NUTRITIONAL CONTENTS:

Calories: 481

Total Fat: 25g

Saturated Fat: 8g

Cholesterol: 469mg

Sodium: 297mg

Total Carbs: 40g

Fiber: 6g

Sugar: 6g

Protein: 25g

Potassium: 1143mg

Curly Fries

Servings: 2 | Temperature: 350°F

Prep Time: 5 minutes | Cook Time: 15 minutes

INGREDIENTS:

- 2 potatoes
- 1 tablespoon extra-virgin olive oil
- 1 teaspoon pepper

- 1 teaspoon salt
- 1 teaspoon paprika

DIRECTIONS:

1. Pre-heat your air fryer to 350°F.

2. Wash potatoes thoroughly and pass them through a spiralizer to get curly shapes.

3. Take a bowl and add potatoes to the bowl, toss and coat well with pepper, salt, oil, and paprika.

4. Transfer the curly fries to air fryer cooking basket and cook for 15 minutes.

5. Sprinkle more salt and paprika, serve and enjoy!

NUTRITIONAL CONTENTS:

Calories: 150
Total Fat: 4g
Saturated Fat: 0g
Cholesterol: 0mg
Sodium: 471mg

Total Carbs: 27g
Fiber: 1g
Sugar: 1g
Protein: 3g
Potassium: 629mg

Garlic Prawn

Servings: 3 | Temperature: 356°F

Prep Time: 5 minutes | Cook Time: 8 minutes

INGREDIENTS:

- 15 fresh prawns
- 1 tablespoon olive oil
- 1 teaspoon chili powder
- 1 tablespoon black pepper

- 1 tablespoon chili sauce
- 1 garlic clove, minced
- Salt as needed

DIRECTIONS:

1. Pre-heat your air fryer to 356°F.

2. Wash prawns thoroughly and rinse them.

3. Take a mixing bowl and add washed prawn, chili powder, oil, garlic, pepper, chili sauce and stir the mix.

4. Transfer prawn to air fryer and cook for 8 minutes.

5. Serve and enjoy!

NUTRITIONAL CONTENTS:

Calories: 131
Total Fat: 10g
Saturated Fat: 1g
Cholesterol: 63mg
Sodium: 286mg

Total Carbs: 4g
Fiber: 1g
Sugar: 1g
Protein: 7g
Potassium: 152mg

Beef Tomato Meatballs

Servings: 6 | Temperature: 390°F and 300°F

Prep Time: 10 minutes | Cook Time: 5 minutes

INGREDIENTS:

- 1 small onion, chopped
- ¾ pounds ground beef
- 1 tablespoon fresh parsley, chopped
- ½ tablespoon fresh thyme leaves, chopped

- 1 whole egg
- 3 tablespoons breadcrumbs
- Salt and pepper to taste
- Tomato sauce

101

DIRECTIONS:

1. Chop onion and keep them on the side.

2. Take a bowl and add listed ingredients, mix well (including onions).

3. Make 12 balls.

4. Pre-heat your air fryer to 390°F, transfer balls to the fryer.

5. Cook for 8 minutes (in batches if needed) and transfer the balls to the oven.

6. Add tomatoes sauce and drown the balls.

7. Transfer the dish to your air fryer and cook for 5 minutes at 300°F.

8. Stir and serve.

9. Enjoy!

NUTRITIONAL CONTENTS:

Calories: 257
Total Fat: 18g
Saturated Fat: 7g
Cholesterol: 82mg
Sodium: 429mg

Total Carbs: 7g
Fiber: 1g
Sugar: 3g
Protein: 15g
Potassium: 432mg

Dessert Recipes

Banana Chips

Servings: 3 | Temperature: 352°F

Prep Time: 5 minutes | Cook Time: 15 minutes

INGREDIENTS:

- 3-4 raw banana
- 1 teaspoon salt
- ½ teaspoon turmeric powder
- ½ teaspoon Chaat Masala
- 1 teaspoon olive oil

DIRECTIONS:

1. Peel the skin of the bananas and keep them gently on the side.

2. Take a bowl and add the turmeric, salt, powder, and water.

3. Cut the banana slices into the mix.

4. Soak for 10 minutes.

5. Drain them out and dry the chips.

6. Drizzle a bit of oil on top of the chips.

7. Pre-heat your fryer to 352°F.

8. Transfer the chips and fry them for 15 minutes.

9. Enjoy!

NUTRITIONAL CONTENTS:

Calories: 307
Total Fat: 14g
Saturated Fat: 8g
Cholesterol: 46mg
Sodium: 164mg

Total Carbs: 42g
Fiber: 3g
Sugar: 26g
Protein: 4g
Potassium: 143mg

Tender Muffin Balls

Servings: 4 | Temperature: 352°F

Prep Time: 5 minutes | Cook Time: 15 minutes

INGREDIENTS:

- 3 ounces plain granola
- 3 handful cooked vegetables of your choice
- ¼ cup coconut milk
- Handful of thyme diced
- 1 tablespoon coriander
- Salt and pepper to taste

DIRECTIONS:

1. Take a mixing bowl and add cooked vegetables.

2. Take an immersion blender and whiz granola until you have a breadcrumb-like texture.

3. Add coconut milk to the granola and add veggies.

4. Mix well into muffin/ball shapes.

5. Transfer them to your air fryer cooking basket and cook for 352°F for 20 minutes.

6. Serve and enjoy!

NUTRITIONAL CONTENTS:

Calories: 138
Total Fat: 8g
Saturated Fat: 5g
Cholesterol: 22mg
Sodium: 199mg

Total Carbs: 15g
Fiber: 2g
Sugar: 1g
Protein: 2g
Potassium: 318mg

Delicious Jalapeno Poppers

Servings: 4 | Temperature: 370°F

Prep Time: 5 minutes | Cook Time: 8 minutes

INGREDIENTS:

- 10 jalapeno poppers, halved and deseeded
- 8 ounces cashew cream
- ¼ cup fresh parsley
- ¾ cup breadcrumbs

DIRECTIONS:

1. Take a bowl and mix ½ of crumbs and cashew cream.

2. Add parsley and stuff the pepper with the mixture.

3. Press the top gently with remaining crumbs and make an even topping.

4. Transfer to air fryer cooking basket and cook for 8 minutes at 370°F.

5. Let it cool and enjoy!

NUTRITIONAL CONTENTS:

Calories: 694
Total Fat: 68g
Saturated Fat: 27g
Cholesterol: 131mg
Sodium: 828mg

Total Carbs: 8g
Fiber: 0g
Sugar: 0g
Protein: 15g
Potassium: 191mg

Air Baked Apples

Servings: 8 | Temperature: 356°F

Prep Time: 5 minutes | Cook Time: 10 minutes

INGREDIENTS:

- 4 apples
- ¾ ounces butter
- 2 tablespoons brown sugar
- 1¾ ounces fresh breadcrumbs
- 1½ ounces mixed seeds
- Zest of 1 orange
- 1 teaspoon cinnamon

DIRECTIONS:

1. Prepare apples by scoring skin around the circumference and coring them using a knife.

2. Take cored apples and stuff the listed ingredients.

3. Pre-heat your Fryer to 356°F.

4. Transfer apples to air fryer basket and bake for 10 minutes.

5. Serve and enjoy!

NUTRITIONAL CONTENTS:

Calories: 152
Total Fat: 2g
Saturated Fat: 1g
Cholesterol: 5mg
Sodium: 2mg

Total Carbs: 35g
Fiber: 5g
Sugar: 27g
Protein: 1g
Potassium: 204mg

Chocolate Soufflé

Servings: 4 | Temperature: 338°F

Prep Time: 10 minutes | Cook Time: 20 minutes

INGREDIENTS:

- 6 tablespoons sugar
- 1½ cups chocolate
- 2 egg yolks
- 4 egg whites

- 1 tablespoon heavy cream
- 1 teaspoon plain flour
- 1 teaspoon ground cinnamon
- 1 teaspoon salt

DIRECTIONS:

1. Pre-heat your air fryer to 338°F. Take 4 ramekins and grease it up well.

2. Coat the inside with 1½ teaspoon of sugar

3. Add chopped up chocolate on top of a double boiler over hot, but not boiling water.

4. Keep stirring until the chocolate has melted.

5. You may also melt the chocolate in your microwave.

6. Take a medium sized bowl and beat your egg whites, salt and 4 tablespoons of sugar.

7. Keep beating it until stiff peak forms.

8. Fold half of the beaten whites into your chocolate mix and keep mixing until a smooth texture forms.

9. Fold the combined mixture back into the remaining egg whites and keep mixing until the white streaks are gone.

10. Divide the mix between the four different ramekins and place them in your air fryer.

11. Let it cook for 15-20 minutes until it is fully inflated and firm to touch.

12. Dust them with some confectioner's sugar if you want.

13. Enjoy the mouthwatering soufflé!

NUTRITIONAL CONTENTS:

Calories: 187
Total Fat: 8g
Saturated Fat: 4g
Cholesterol: 98mg
Sodium: 47mg

Total Carbs: 28g
Fiber: 2g
Sugar: 23g
Protein: 5g
Potassium: 164mg

Caramel Sauce & Brownie

Servings: 5　|　Temperature: 356°F

Prep Time: 5 minutes　|　Cook Time: 15 minutes

INGREDIENTS:

- 4 ounces caster sugar
- 2 tablespoons water
- ½ cup milk
- 4 ounces butter

- 2 ounces chocolate
- 6 ounces brown sugar
- 2 thoroughly beaten eggs
- 2 teaspoons vanilla essence

DIRECTIONS:

1. Pre-heat your air fryer to 356°F.

2. Take a bowl and add butter, chocolate.

3. Pour mixture into the pan and place it over medium heat.

4. Take a bowl and add beaten eggs, sugar, vanilla essence, raising flour and mix well.

5. Take a dish and grease it.

6. Pour beaten egg mixture into the dish.

7. Transfer dish to the air fryer cooking basket and cook for 15 minutes.

8. Take another pan and add caster sugar, heat until melted.

9. Stir in butter into caramel and let it melt.

10. Top brownies with caramel and enjoy!

NUTRITIONAL CONTENTS:

Calories: 276
Total Fat: 12g
Saturated Fat: 7g
Cholesterol: 57mg
Sodium: 124mg

Total Carbs: 39g
Fiber: 2g
Sugar: 30g
Protein: 3g
Potassium: 100mg

Almond Apple Bites

Servings: 4 | Temperature: 360°F

Prep Time: 15 minutes | Cook Time: 20 minutes

INGREDIENTS:

- 4 apples
- 1½ ounces almonds
- Whipped cream as needed
- ¾ ounces raisins
- 2 tablespoon sugar

DIRECTIONS:

1. Pre-heat your air fryer to 360°F.

2. Wash apples and clean them, cut off the core.

3. Take and mix in sugar, almonds, raisins, blend using a blender.

4. Fill apples with the prepared mixture.

5. Transfer to air fryer cooking basket and cook for 10 minutes.

6. Serve with powdered sugar, enjoy!

NUTRITIONAL CONTENTS:

Calories: 406
Total Fat: 20g
Saturated Fat: 3g
Cholesterol: 57mg
Sodium: 289mg

Total Carbs: 51g
Fiber: 3g
Sugar: 34g
Protein: 8g
Potassium: 193mg

Conventional Oven to Air Fryer Conversion

	Cooking Temperature	Cooking Time
Conventional Oven	200 F	30 min
Air Fryer	185 F (100 C)	24 min

Cooking Times

	Time, min	Temperature, F
Poultry		
Breasts, Legs, Thighs (bone in)	25 -30	380
Breasts (boneless), Wings	12	380
Drumsticks	20	370
Tenders	10	360
Whole Chicken	75	360

Meat		
Meatballs	8-10	380
Burger	18	370
Beefsteak	12	400
Pork Chops	12	400
Bacon	8	400
Sausages	15	380
Lamb Chops	10	400

Fish & Seafood		
Fish Fillet	10	400
Calamari	4	400
Scallops, Shrimp	6	400

Vegetables		
Asparagus	5	400
Broccoli	6	400
Carrots	15	380
Mushrooms	5	400

Onion	10	400
Peppers	15	400
Potatoes	12	400
Tomatoes	4-10	400
Frozen Foods		
Onion Rings	8	400
Mozarella Sticks	8	400
Chicken Nuggets	10	400
Breaded Shrimp	9	400
Fish Sticks	10	400

About the Author

A **professional cook**, Christopher Lester has made a name for himself on **innovative cooking techniques and a commitment to flavor and health** above all else. He has learned from and collaborated with some of the biggest culinary names in the South, accruing a treasure trove of tools and techniques that give his recipes and dishes tastes that are full, rich, and unique.

Working as a chef, he spends a lot of time in the kitchen, and **he particularly enjoys cooking in an air fryer.**

A father of two, Christopher also shares his home with the family dog, Jack. Christopher finds joy in teaching his kids about delicious, wholesome cooking.

One of his favorite pastimes is cooking for his loved ones, gathering up his friends and family for elaborate dinners at which he can put all his cooking skills to good use.

Our Recommendations

  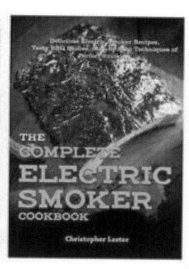

If you have a free minute, please leave your review of the book. Your feedback is essential for us, as well as for other readers.

Recipe Index

Copyright

Printed in Great Britain
by Amazon